RUNNING WITH RACHEL

RUNNING WITH RACHEL

BY FRANK AND JAN ASCH

PHOTOGRAPHS BY JAN ASCH
AND ROBERT MICHAEL BUSLOW

THE DIAL PRESS   New York

Published by
The Dial Press
1 Dag Hammarskjold Plaza
New York, New York 10017

Text copyright © 1979 by Frank and Jan Asch
Photographs copyright © 1979 by
Jan Asch and Robert Michael Buslow
All rights reserved. Manufactured in the U.S.A.
First printing. Designed by Jane Byers Bierhorst

Library of Congress Cataloging in Publication Data

Asch, Frank.
Running with Rachel.

Summary: Rachel discusses running, including how her interest began, proper shoes, diet, exercises, and competition.
1. Jogging—Juvenile literature. 2. Running—Juvenile literature. [1. Running] I. Asch, Jan, joint author. II. Buslow, Robert Michael. III. Title.
GV494.A75   796.4'26   78-72471
ISBN 0-8037-7553-9 lib. bdg.
ISBN 0-8037-7552-0 pbk.

to Mom

GETTING STARTED

One day I was riding my bike and I saw a woman running down the road. She was wearing bright blue shorts with a stripe down the side, funny green sneakers, and heavy socks. I turned to look and skidded on some loose gravel.

I went flying over the handlebars and landed in a ditch. I wasn't hurt much, just scraped up a bit. My bike wasn't so lucky. The front wheel was so bent out of shape it was impossible to ride home. I could hardly push it. Then the woman in the bright blue shorts came over to me.

"Hey, are you okay?" she asked.

"I guess so. But look at my bike!"

"Can I give you a hand with it?"

"Sure," I said, and she helped me push the bike all the way home.

"What's your name?" she asked.

"Rachel," I said. "What's yours?"

"Cathy," she replied.

Cathy was very easy to talk to. I told her all about my dollhouse collection and my guinea pigs, and she told me about her new job and vegetable garden. And of course I wanted to know why she'd been running down the road!

When we got to my house, my dog came to greet us. Cathy knelt down to pet him and got licked in the face.

"I'll bet you get chased by a lot of dogs," I said.

"It happens sometimes," she replied. "The little ones I tell to go home in a firm voice, and the big ones I try to ignore."

"And what if that doesn't work?" I asked.

"Then," she said, smiling, "I run a little faster."

My mom offered Cathy a glass of water and we talked some more, mostly about running. I had a lot of questions and Cathy didn't mind answering them.

"How did you get started?" I asked.

"I bought myself a good pair of running shoes," she said, "and just started running. I began with a quarter mile and then built up slowly to give my body a chance to adjust. In a few weeks I was up to a mile. Now it's been several months, and I run at least three miles a day."

"Isn't there more to it than just having a good pair of running shoes?" asked my mother.

"Well," said Cathy, "there *are* some basic commonsense things, like not running right after you eat, and doing a few warm-up exercises to stretch your muscles so you don't hurt yourself. Another thing that's important is to use your whole foot when you run, landing on your heel, rolling to the ball of your foot, and pushing off with your toes. What that does is help distribute the shock evenly and prevent knee injuries."

"And that's it?" asked my mom skeptically.

"Really, if you're just running for the fun of it, it's not that complicated. But of course if you're overweight or think there might be some medical complication, you should see your doctor before you begin."

"Running's not for me," said my mom. "I like accomplishing something when I exercise, like working in the garden."

"Oh, you have a garden?" exclaimed Cathy. "So do I."

My mom loves to show off her garden, so that was the last I saw of them until Cathy had to leave.

"Thanks a lot for helping me with my bike," I shouted after her.

"See you around," she said as she jogged down the road.

A TRIAL RUN

I've always liked running. Whenever I have a choice between running and walking, like to the store for my mom or just from the front door to the school bus, I always choose running. Walking takes too much time, and running just feels better. I've never enjoyed running at school though; they always make such a big deal about who's the fastest. I got the feeling that the way Cathy ran was lots more fun.

Later that week I got home from school a bit frazzled. My most unfavorite teacher, Mr. P, gave an awful quiz, Miss C said "UH" eighty-nine times, and I spilled clam chowder on my favorite shirt.

I turned on the TV but there was nothing on except soap operas. I looked at my schoolbooks sitting on the dining-room table and cringed. My mind was racing around in five different directions, and my body felt like a lump. I felt itchy—but on the inside!

I decided to go for a run.

I ran out the front door, down the driveway, and up the street. At the corner I ran across the baseball field and around the pond where a few kids were fishing. Then I ran away from all the houses and into the fields. It was the end of May and lots of flowers were already blooming.

I felt my heart pounding and the blood rushing through my veins. Everything in my body was saying:

"Hey, where ya been all day? We missed you."

My shadow loped along with me and fell across the spring-green grass that was growing redder as the sun set. I ran the way Cathy had showed me, rolling forward from my heel to my toe, but I still had on my school shoes, and they were starting to hurt. I ignored the pain and picked up speed.

Mr. P's surprise quiz seemed far away from me now. So did Miss C and Mr. D, and Miss W. I imagined the whole bunch of them in wheelchairs trying to chase me across the field. I turned my head to look and pretended they were so far behind I couldn't even see them.

I looked down at my shadow. It seemed alive to me. I wondered if I could stop suddenly and catch it off guard. Would it run ahead a few paces? I picked up a little more speed and imagined that I could outrun my shadow.

By now my feet were really hurting. I slowed down to a jog and then to a walk. My heart was still pounding. My arms and legs felt tingly, like blood was flowing to places it had never gone before.

I sat down and took my shoes off to see what the damages were.

"Congratulations!" I told myself. "You are the proud mother of several baby blisters."

My feet hurt, but I knew I could get good shoes and take care of that. What mattered was that that itchy-on-the-inside feeling was gone now.

As I limped home, I wondered how Mom was going to take the news that I needed a new pair of shoes—running shoes.

RUNNING SHOES

Mom took the news just fine. In fact a few days later we went downtown to buy my first pair of running shoes. First we tried a few shoe stores, but they didn't have a very good selection. Then we went to a sports shop. The salesman there seemed to know a lot about what we needed.

"Basically what you should look for in a jogging shoe," he said, "is a sole that's cushioned and flexible. It should have a heel that is somewhat raised—about the same as a street shoe."

Mom insisted that they have good arch supports. The salesman agreed.

I tried on a few pairs. The first pair was so heavy it made me feel like Bigfoot. The next pair was nice and light but too tight in the toes. The third pair seemed to fit better. "It's important that they feel comfortable," said the salesman.

Mom helped me lace up the shoes and I jogged up and down the aisle of the store.

"They feel comfortable," I said, "very comfortable."

"Good," said the salesman. "If they get wet, stuff them with newspaper and let them dry out slowly, never over heat." He put my old shoes in a box and handed them to the cashier.

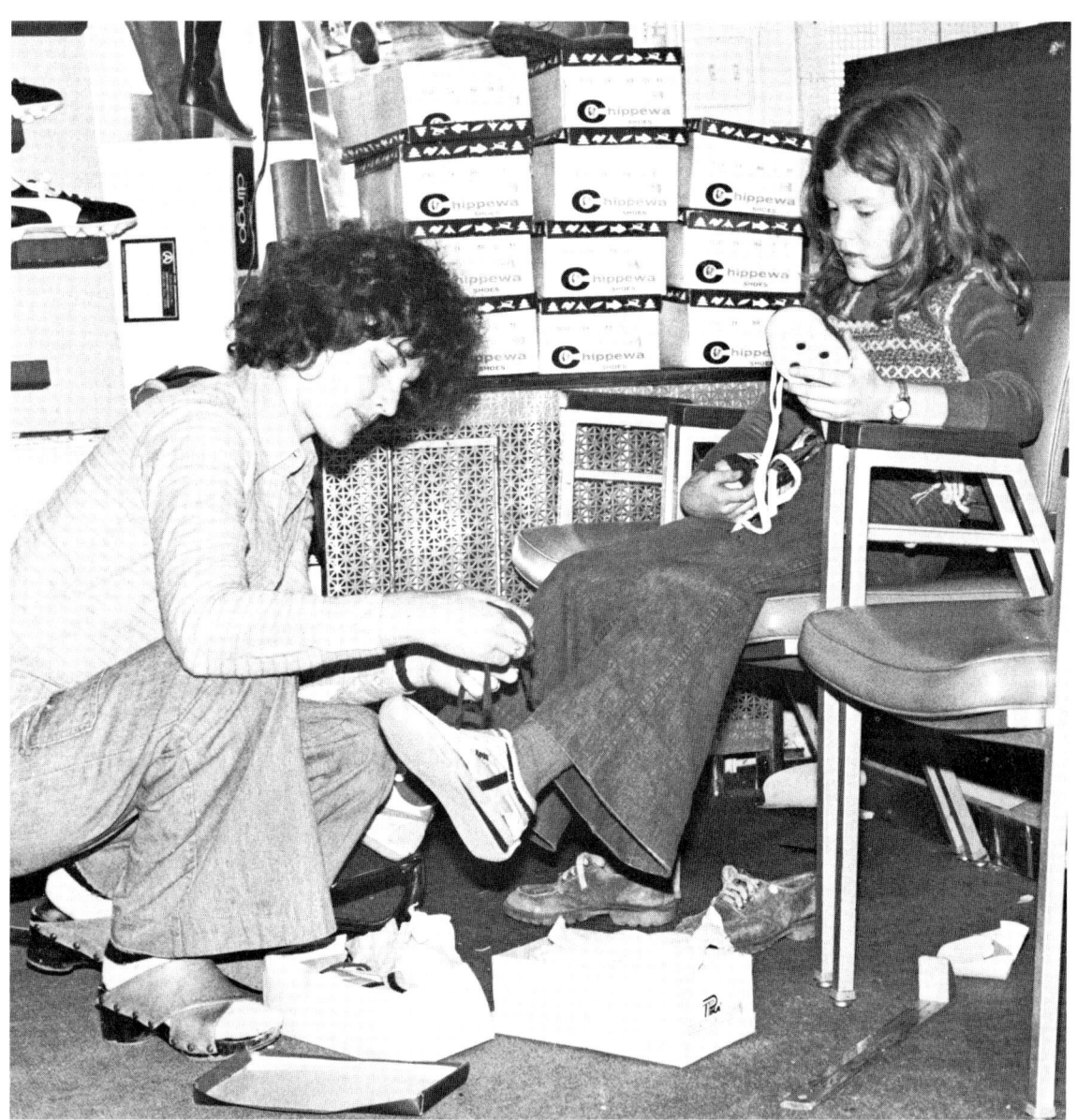

"Did you want some running shorts to go with them? We have them on sale right now."

I looked at my mom, and she said it was okay. I picked out two pairs and a T-shirt too. I tried everything on and looked at myself in the mirror. It was the new me—the running me. I felt official, and so good.

"I'll meet you at the car," I yelled to Mom and took off down the street like a pebble from a slingshot.

My new shoes really made me feel important, and somehow, a better, faster runner. My feet felt so light and sure as they gripped the pavement. I tried to use my whole foot the way Cathy had said, and it felt great. I leaped up and down curbs and stopped on a dime at the traffic light. I knew it would take my mom a while to pay the bill and walk to the car, so I took the long route.

As I ran through the park, the squirrels picked up their heads. I could see and feel springtime all around.

When I got to the car, Mom was already there.

That night I wrote in my diary.

Dear Diary,

Today I got my first pair of running shoes. They're blue and white, and so soft they make my feet feel like they're wrapped in clouds. They were kind of expensive, but Mom wanted to get me good ones. She didn't say anything, but I can tell she's afraid I'll lose interest in running and they will be just so much wasted money. But I don't think she has to worry. I like running as much as my dollhouse and my guinea pigs too!

P.S. Three more weeks till school is out.

YIPPIE!!!

LIBRARY
ATLANTIC CHRISTIAN COLLEGE
WILSON, N. C.

MORE TIPS FROM CATHY

The next day was Saturday. I got up early, put on my new shoes and shorts, and went for a run. I was hoping to see Cathy again, so I ran back and forth past the spot where we first met. Finally she came running down the road. She seemed as pleased to see me as I was to see her.

We sat down on the grass and talked for a while. She wanted to hear everything about my new interest in running and offered to show me some warm-up exercises.

"You'll probably want to add or subtract a few according to your own needs," she said.

"What do you mean, my own needs?" I asked.

"Some people are more stiff in the hips, others in the knees. You'll want to do exercises that loosen up the places where you need it most."

"Okay," I said. "How do we begin?"

"Well, I always start with some leg stretching. Bend your standing leg and put the other leg back, keeping your knee straight. Lean forward a little, putting your weight on the leg that's bent."

"Like this?" I asked.

"Good. Now switch legs."

I could feel my muscles stretching like a new rubberband.

"Boy, did I need that," I said.

"Be careful not to strain," warned Cathy.

"I see what you mean about certain places needing exercise more than others. That one is hard for me!"

"Leg-stretching exercises are very important," Cathy told me, "because running puts so much strain on the legs."

"What's next?" I asked.

"Forward bending. Just bend at the waist and try to touch your toes."

I could touch my toes right away. Then I stretched a little more and touched the ground with my fingertips, then with the palms of my hands. It didn't hurt at all.

"That one's easier," I said.

Next we did some trunk twisting.

"Stand with your feet spread apart, arms out to the sides, like this," she demonstrated. "Okay, now slowly turn from side to side, but keep your feet in place."

"Did you hear that, Cathy?"

"What?"

"My back just made a cracking sound."

"Mine does that sometimes too," she said.

Trunk twisting was the easiest of all, and it made my back feel really good.

"Now this time bend to the sides. Keep your arms out and bend to the right. Try to hold on to your right leg while you stretch your other arm overhead. Good. Now switch sides."

"That one stretches my sides and my legs too."

Then Cathy sat down on the grass.

"Here's an exercise that's fun," she said. "Lie on your back, arms over your head, and bring your legs up overhead and your toes to your palms. Don't bend your knees."

"It looks silly," I said. "But it really feels comfortable."

"That one is good for your neck and legs," she said.

"What about sit-ups, jumping jacks, and all of those kinds of exercises we do in gym?" I asked.

"Those are good too," said Cathy. "Just experiment. Soon you'll find the exercises that suit you best."

After ten or fifteen minutes of warm-up exercises we were almost ready to run, but first I asked Cathy to give me a few pointers on form.

"Well, basically, just remember to keep your back more or less straight and your shoulders level. Don't hunch over. Your lungs will be able to expand more that way. Keep your forearms parallel to the ground and your hands loosely clenched. No fists. Another thing I learned recently is to 'sit down' when I run."

"What do you mean 'sit down,'" I said.

"Bend your knees just a little so it looks like you're going to sit down. That way your legs can extend farther and your stride is much longer."

I laughed. "Do you really expect me to remember all that?"

"No," she said, "you'll go crazy and end up hating running if you try to get everything right the first time. Just concentrate on one thing at a time and let your body put it all together for you."

Now we were ready to run. I wanted to go fast right away, but Cathy insisted that we start out slowly and build up. Every once in a while she looked over at me.

"You're clenching your fists," she said. "Relax your hands!"

I imitated her motion, flicking my wrists like limp rags while I ran.

"That's it," she said. "Now you've got it."

After a while we built up speed. We ran for half a mile or so and then she walked me the rest of the way home.

"You should always do some sort of warm-down so you don't stiffen up after a run," she advised. "Walking is good, or try some of the same exercises I showed you before."

As we said good-bye, Cathy asked me how I liked my first running lesson. I told her I'd really enjoyed it and thanked her for all the tips. We agreed to get together again sometime.

WHAT I EAT

Weeks went by and school got out. To me that meant no more homework, lots of swimming, and running too. Running every day became a habit that I needed and liked. I ran in the morning before breakfast or in the evening when it cooled off a little. I ran longer distances and felt stronger all the time. One day my dad asked me how far I ran in miles. I didn't really know, so we clocked it in the car. It was almost two miles. Boy, was I proud of myself.

Running not only changed how I felt about myself but it changed how I looked too. I used to have a pot belly and was afraid of becoming overweight. I remember one day we went to the planetarium. There were scales there that told you how much you weigh on other planets. When I found out I weighed only sixteen pounds on the moon, I thought to myself, "If I ever get fat, I'll go there to live." People were starting to tease me about my pot belly, and I was thinking of going on a diet, but after two months of running there was no need to. I just burned off that extra weight.

Running makes me sweat a lot so I have to drink more water or fresh fruit juice, especially in hot weather. I also take some vitamins—B, C, and a multiple vitamin.

Running has even changed what I eat—nothing fancy, but I really try to eat good stuff. Sometimes while I eat, I picture the food going into my body, building me up, and making me stronger.

For breakfast I usually have eggs and toast, or granola with fruit and milk. I guess in the winter I'll go back to hot oatmeal with raisins, walnuts, and honey—my favorite.

A garden salad is nice for lunch on a hot day or when I don't feel like having my usual—a sandwich. My favorites are tuna fish and tomato, and cheese and alfalfa sprouts. Sometimes I mix fresh fruit and plain yogurt in the blender and freeze it to make yogurt popsicles. They're great! For dinner Mom usually cooks meat or fish and always lots of fresh vegetables. Lately, heavy greasy foods like french fries and hamburgers just don't appeal to me as much as they used to, and I don't eat so many snack foods or sweets.

When I go shopping with Mom in the supermarket we always get fresh or at least frozen vegetables and never the canned kind. They always look like they've been sitting there since the day you were born!

Lately I've really come to appreciate my mom's garden. She grows everything there organically, and you sure can taste the difference.

I've even started growing my own alfalfa sprouts. It's not difficult at all. I just soak the seeds overnight in a large glass jar. In the morning I drain the water and cover the jar with cheesecloth and set it in a dark place. I rinse them two or three times a day. When they get to be about three quarters of an inch long, I move them into the sunlight for another day or so until they turn green. Then they're ready for salads or sandwiches. Mmm!

RUN FOR FUN

People don't tease me about getting fat anymore, but sometimes they tease me about running itself. They say things like "If you keep running so much, you're going to have muscles like a boy." Of course that's not true. Other times they say things like "What's new with the latest fad?" That gets me very angry.

Most people, however, are very encouraging. My mom and dad are always bragging about me and even talk about taking up running themselves. Lots of times people are amazed that I manage to keep up my interest and sometimes so am I. It's so much easier to flop down and watch TV than to put on my running shoes and shorts and exercise or go out for a run. Sometimes I have to remind myself how good I'll feel afterward. I try to make it easy for myself by keeping my shoes and shorts handy. I also keep up my interest by exploring new places to run.

Running has a lonely side. I often talk to myself or even to certain landmarks like familiar trees and fire hydrants, saying, "Hello, how are you? How's your paint job?"

Sometimes when I'm running down the road someone will shout out something dumb like:

"Faster, faster," or "Hey, girlie, get a horse."

Things like that make you feel even lonelier.

All summer I kept hoping to find someone my age to run with, but everyone I know who runs is quite a bit older or interested more in racing than just running. Then one day my dad showed me an ad in the paper:

RUN FOR FUN, COME ONE, COME ALL!
THREE AGE CATEGORIES
one-mile race ages 9–12
two-mile race ages 12–16
three-mile race ages 16 and up
registration fee—50¢

The idea didn't appeal to me until my dad suggested that I might meet a running buddy there.

When the day of the race came, I got Mom to take me down to the local high school where the race was to be held. It was already August and the football team was starting to practice. I looked around and saw only a few kids my age and, what was worse, I was the only girl. By the time I had finished my warm-ups, there were a few more kids, but still no girls. While my mom massaged my legs for me to get them nice and limber, I had what I call one of my Bionic Woman fantasies. In the fantasy I outrun all the boys. The judges are amazed and give me a special award, but I humbly refuse.

My mom paid my fifty-cent entrance fee. Then the man who was in charge of the race, a young guy with a coach's cap and a stopwatch, called everyone over to the starting line. A woman took down our names and pointed out the course for us.

"It's twice around the entire athletic field." She motioned with her arm. "There'll be someone running along with you to let you know exactly where the course goes. If you get tired, don't hesitate to stop. Remember, it's run for *fun*."

There were only about nine of us on the starting line. My mom kept saying, "Now, take it easy, Rachel."

The race began. I knew I didn't have much of a chance of winning; I just wanted to do my best. And I guess I have to admit I didn't want to come in last. I turned and saw a couple of guys way behind me and I relaxed. There was another kid running ahead of me kind of slow. I surprised myself and passed him effortlessly.

Somewhere in the middle of the race, around the first lap, my shoes came untied...both of them at once. I ran a few hundred feet to where my mother was and she helped me tie them. It felt like forever until they were tied, and of course I wasn't ahead anymore.

As I came around the final turn, I heard some of the other parents shouting out things like "Come on, they're catching up," and "Get the lead out," but my mom was still shouting "Take it easy, Rachel."

As soon as I came across the finish line, she gave me a big hug. One kid ahead of me had pushed himself so hard, he was limping and holding his side in agony. Another kid was really desperate to find out what his time had been.

"What's my time, what's my time," he kept saying.

"Three seconds better than last time," they told him.

But that didn't seem to be good enough for him.

"Next time I'll do better, you'll see. I'll cut down my time six more seconds."

I looked at my mom and she looked at me. I knew we were both thinking the same thing. "So this is Run for Fun."

We moved away from the crowd and I did some warm-down exercises. I leaned forward and let all of the tension flow out of me.

Then something really nice happened. A girl my age dressed in running clothes came over to me and introduced herself.

"My name is Randy," she said. "We're kind of new in this area and my dad got lost on the way so I missed the race."

I told her my name and asked her where she lived. It turned out to be very close to my neighborhood. Then I got really excited!

"Would you like to run together sometime?" I asked.

She said she'd love to.

"Ready, Rachel?" interrupted my mother. "I'd like to get home soon."

We quickly exchanged phone numbers and said good-bye.

RUNNING WITH RANDY

When I got home, my dad asked me how the race was.

"Just great," I told him and gave him a big kiss.

That night after dinner I was just about to pick up the phone to call Randy when the phone rang.... It was Randy calling me!

"I was just going to call you," I said, and we both giggled. It was the beginning of a lot of giggling.

The next day we went for our first run together. Some of the warm-ups that she did were a lot like the ones Cathy showed me. Others were very different.

"I get tired of doing the same exercises all the time, don't you?" asked Randy.

"Yeah," I agreed. "Let's make up some of our own."

Suddenly Randy started jumping on one foot.

"This one I call the bunny rabbit," she said. "It helps relieve tension around the nose."

At last I found someone as silly as I am, I thought to myself.

One day Randy came over to my house, and after her visit I decided to run her home. When we got to her house, she decided to run me home. We went back and forth that way a couple of times giggling all the way. Neither of us could stop. Finally it got dark and we decided to say good-bye halfway between her house and my house.

We found that running and Frisbee were a good combination. But usually while we ran we talked.

"Did you ever think about running in a marathon?" I once asked Randy.

"Absolutely," she said. "We'll run the entire twenty-six miles backward."

"No, really," I insisted. "What do you think about it?"

"Well," she replied, "I think you're supposed to train for about a year or so first."

"Maybe my friend Cathy will train us," I said. Randy liked that idea just fine.

If it started raining while we were running, we kept on going as long as there was no thunder or lightning. Our clothes got drenched, but we loved it. When the rain stopped, we took off our shoes and ran through puddles.

Sometimes the summer weather was too hot, and we didn't run at all. Then in September the weather cooled off and we started running longer distances. One day we decided to run four miles.

The first mile we were feeling very strong. After the second mile we both started feeling like we weren't going to make it.

"You want to stop?" asked Randy.

"No," I said, "let's just slow down and keep going."

Luckily at that point the road started to go downhill. We picked up speed and both of us got a second wind.

We finished the four miles with ease, thanks to that hill, and could have run even farther but we were both afraid of straining ourselves and risking a cramp.

RUNNING ON

When Randy was sick or too busy to run with me, I would still run alone. I didn't mind at all. In fact, now that I had a friend to run with, I found myself looking forward to those times when I *could* run alone. I *liked* not having to keep up or slow down for anyone; but more than that, sometimes I liked just being alone.

When I run alone, I can really pay attention to things like the feel of the wind against my face and the look of everything flying past in straight lines, colors, all mixing in a blur. Then it's easier to fall into the rhythm of my body and the sound of my shoes hitting the ground.

There are times when I like to look at the scenery and just let my mind run on. I think about all kinds of things like entering my guinea pigs in the 4-H fair or what to get my parents for their anniversary. Other times I like to forget about everything and just put myself completely into my body. I put myself in my feet and legs for a while and then move up to my stomach, shoulders, and arms. The more I run, the less my body feels like a bunch of pieces all stuck together. When I'm running well, my arms aren't just arms anymore; they feel powerful and alive like train wheels or pistons in a big engine, and my hair flying behind me isn't just hair, but something special like a horse's mane or a blazing fire.

When I run alone, I run at my own pace, sometimes slowly, stopping to smell a flower or to look at the sunset. Sometimes I like to run fast, far and fast. Then I flop onto the ground and listen to the sounds and the silence and watch the clouds drift by.

ABOUT THE AUTHORS

Frank Asch is described by *Publishers Weekly* as "a singularly gifted contributor to children's literature." He is the author of *MacGooses' Grocery* (Dial) and *Yellow, Yellow,* and the author/illustrator of *Turtle Tale* (Dial). Mr. Asch's many other vocations and avocations include children's theater and abstract painting. He and his wife, Jan, with whom he collaborated on *Running With Rachel,* live in Brooklyn, Connecticut.

Jan Asch grew up in New Rochelle, New York, and was graduated from Rosemont College in Pennsylvania. She formerly taught in a Montessori nursery school, and she is also a storyteller, songwriter, and musician. This is her first book.

Robert Michael Buslow was born in New York City and grew up in Brooklyn, Connecticut. He is a graduate of Rhode Island School of Photography. A veteran free-lance photographer, Mr. Buslow is also staff photographer and instructor at the New England Center for Contemporary Art in Brooklyn, Connecticut.